Strangers No Longer

Together on the Journey of Hope

A PASTORAL LETTER CONCERNING MIGRATION
FROM THE CATHOLIC BISHOPS OF MEXICO AND THE UNITED STATES

United States Conference of Catholic Bishops
Washington, D.C.

The document *Strangers No Longer: Together on the Journey of Hope* was developed by the Committee on Migration of the United States Conference of Catholic Bishops (USCCB) in collaboration with the Conferencia del Episcopado Mexicano (CEM). It was approved simultaneously by the full bodies of U.S. Catholic bishops and the Mexican bishops at their November 2002 General Meetings and has been authorized for publication in the United States by the undersigned.

Msgr. William P. Fay
General Secretary, USCCB

Photos credits: cover, p. vi, © CRDphoto/CORBIS; p. 4, Adveniat; pp. 7 and 8, © David Turnley/CORBIS; p. 10, Colleen O'Neill, *West Nebraska Register*/CNS; p. 17, © David H. Wells/CORBIS; p. 18, Tommy Bassett; p. 21, © Jonathan Blair/CORBIS; p. 24, Bob Roller/CNS; p. 27, Br. Ed Dunn; p. 29, Royalty-Free/CORBIS; p. 30, © AFP/CORBIS; p. 43, Reuters/CNS.

Photo on page 30 shows former Foreign Secretary of Mexico Jorge G. Castañeda with U.S. Secretary of State Colin L. Powell.

Quote from the Second Vatican Council document *Lumen Gentium* (Constitution on the Church) is taken from the English translation first printed by the National Catholic Welfare Conference (now United States Conference of Catholic Bishops) in November 1964.

Quotes from Pope Pius XII's *Exsul Familia* (*On the Spiritual Care to Migrants*) are taken from *The Church's Magna Charta for Migrants*, ed. Rev. Giulivo Tessarolo, PSSC (Staten Island, N.Y.: St. Charles Seminary, 1962). Used with permission. Copies of this book are available from the Center for Migration Studies at the St. Charles Mission Center; phone: 718-351-8800.

First Printing, January 2003

ISBN 1-57455-529-4

Contents

Strangers No Longer

Together on the Journey of Hope

Introduction

1. As we begin the third millennium, we give thanks to God the Father for the many blessings of creation, and to our Lord Jesus Christ for the gift of salvation. We raise our prayer to the Holy Spirit to strengthen and guide us in carrying out all that the Lord has commanded us. In discerning the signs of the times, we note the greatly increased migration among the peoples of the Americas, and we see in this but one manifestation of a worldwide phenomenon—often called globalization—which brings with it great promises along with multiple challenges.

2. We speak as two episcopal conferences but as one Church, united in the view that migration between our two nations is necessary and beneficial. At the same time, some aspects of the migrant experience are far from the vision of the Kingdom of God that Jesus proclaimed: many persons who seek to migrate are suffering, and, in some cases, tragically dying; human rights are abused; families are kept apart; and racist and xenophobic attitudes remain.

3. On January 23, 1999, at the Basilica of Our Lady of Guadalupe, Pope John Paul II presented his apostolic exhortation *Ecclesia in America*, which resulted from the Synod of Bishops of America.[1] In the spirit of ecclesial solidarity begun in that synod and promoted in *Ecclesia in America*, and aware of the migration reality our two nations live, we the bishops of Mexico and the United States seek to awaken our peoples to the mysterious presence of the crucified and risen Lord in the person of the migrant and to renew in them the values of the Kingdom of God that he proclaimed.

4. As pastors to more than ninety million Mexican Catholics and sixty-five million U.S. Catholics, we witness the human consequences of migration in the

life of society every day. We witness the vulnerability of our people involved in all sides of the migration phenomenon, including families devastated by the loss of loved ones who have undertaken the migration journey and children left alone when parents are removed from them. We observe the struggles of landowners and enforcement personnel who seek to preserve the common good without violating the dignity of the migrant. And we share in the concern of religious and social service providers who, without violating civil law, attempt to respond to the migrant knocking at the door.

5. Migrants and immigrants are in our parishes and in our communities. In both our countries, we see much injustice and violence against them and much suffering and despair among them because civil and church structures are still inadequate to accommodate their basic needs.

6. We judge ourselves as a community of faith by the way we treat the most vulnerable among us. The treatment of migrants challenges the consciences of elected officials, policymakers, enforcement officers, residents of border communities, and providers of legal aid and social services, many of whom share our Catholic faith.

7. In preparing this statement we have spoken with migrants, public officials, enforcement officers, social justice activists, pastors, parishioners, and community leaders in both the United States and Mexico as part of a process that lasted two years. Our dialogue has revealed a common desire for a more orderly system that accommodates the reality of migration and promotes just application of civil law. We seek to measure the interests of all parties in the migration phenomenon against the guidelines of Catholic social teaching and to offer a moral framework for embracing, not rejecting, the reality of migration between our two nations. We invite Catholics and persons of good will in both nations to exercise their faith and to use their resources and gifts to truly welcome the stranger among us (cf. Mt 25:35).

8. In recent years, signs of hope have developed in the migration phenomenon in both Mexico and the United States: a growing consciousness of migrants as bearers of faith and culture; an outpouring of hospitality and social services, including migrant shelters; a growing network of advocates for migrants' and immigrants' rights; a more organized effort at welcome and intercultural communion; a greater development of a social conscience; and greater recognition by both governments of the importance of the issue of migration. Each of our episcopal conferences has spoken with great urgency to encourage these signs of hope.[2] We reiterate our appreciation for and our encouragement of manifestations of commitment to solidarity according to the vision inspired by *Ecclesia in America* (EA).

9. We speak to the migrants who are forced to leave their lands to provide for their families or to escape persecution. We stand in solidarity with you. We commit ourselves to your pastoral care and to work toward changes in church and societal structures that impede your exercising your dignity and living as children of God.

10. We speak to public officials in both nations, from those who hold the highest offices to those who encounter the migrant on a daily basis. We thank our nations' presidents for the dialogue they have begun in an effort to humanize the migration phenomenon.

11. We speak to government personnel of both countries who enforce, implement, and execute the immigration laws.

12. Finally, we speak to the peoples of the United States and Mexico. Our two nations are more interdependent than ever before in our history, sharing cultural and social values, common interests, and hopes for the future. Our nations have a singular opportunity to act as true neighbors and to work together to build a more just and generous immigration system.

CHAPTER I

America: A Common History of Migration and a Shared Faith in Jesus Christ

13. America is a continent born of immigrant peoples who came to inhabit these lands and who from north to south gave birth to new civilizations. Throughout history the continent has suffered through the expansion of other peoples who came to conquer and colonize these lands, displacing and eliminating entire peoples and even forcing unknown millions of persons and families from Africa to come as slaves.

14. It was precisely within the historical processes of forced and voluntary movements that faith in Christ entered into these lands and extended all over the continent. Faith in Christ has thus "shaped [our] religious profile, marked by moral values which, though they are not always consistently practiced and at times are cast into doubt, are in a sense the heritage of all Americans, even of those who do not explicitly recognize this fact" (EA, no. 14).

15. Our continent has consistently received immigrants, refugees, exiles, and the persecuted from other lands. Fleeing injustice and oppression and seeking liberty and the opportunity to achieve a full life, many have found work, homes, security, liberty, and growth for themselves and their families. Our countries share this immigrant experience, though with different expressions and to different degrees.

16. Since its origins, the Mexican nation has had a history marked by encounters between peoples who, coming from different lands, have transformed and enriched it. It was the encounter between Spaniards and indigenous people that gave rise to the Mexican nation in a birth that was full of the pain and joy that the struggle for life entails. Besides this, immigrants from all continents have participated in the birth of Mexico; they continue to do so now and will for years to come. Mexico is not only a country of *emigrants*, but also a country of *immigrants* who come to build their lives anew. It is important to remember the difficult experiences many of our brothers and sisters have of being strangers in a new land and to welcome those who come to be among us.

17. Since its founding, the United States has received immigrants from around the world who have found opportunity and safe haven in a new land. The labor, values, and beliefs of immigrants from throughout the world have transformed the United States from a loose group of colonies into one of the leading democracies in the world today. From its founding to the present, the United States remains a nation of immigrants grounded in the firm belief that newcomers offer new energy, hope, and cultural diversity.

18. At the present time, the interdependence and integration of our two peoples is clear. According to U.S. government statistics, about 800,000 Mexicans enter the United States each day.[3] Cross-border U.S. and Mexican investment has reached unprecedented levels in recent years. Moreover, each year the United States admits between 150,000 to 200,000 Mexicans into the country as legal permanent residents, amounting to nearly 20 percent of the total number of legal permanent residents *admitted* each year.[4] A significant number of U.S. citizens live, work, and retire in Mexico. In addition to this present interdependence, Mexico and the United States have been bound historically by spiritual connections.

19. Our common faith in Jesus Christ moves us to search for ways that favor a spirit of solidarity. It is a faith that transcends borders and bids us to overcome all forms of discrimination and violence so that we may build relationships that are just and loving.

20. Under the light of the apparition of Our Lady of Guadalupe to the littlest of her children, who were as powerless as most migrants are today, our continent's past and present receive new meaning. It was St. Juan Diego whom our Mother asked to build a temple so in it she could show her love, compassion, aid, and defense to all her children, especially the least among them.[5] Since

then, in her Basilica and beyond its walls, she has brought all the peoples of America to celebrate at the table of the Lord, where all his children may partake of and enjoy the unity of the continent in the diversity of its peoples, languages, and cultures (EA, no. 11).

21. As Pope John Paul II wrote in *Ecclesia in America*:

> In its history, America has experienced many immigrations, as waves of men and women came to its various regions in the hope of a better future. The phenomenon continues even today, especially with many people and families from Latin American countries who have moved to the northern parts of the continent, to the point where in some cases they constitute a substantial part of the population. They often bring with them a cultural and religious heritage which is rich in Christian elements. The Church is well aware of the problems created by this situation and is committed to spare no effort in developing her own pastoral strategy among these immigrant people, in order to help them settle in their new land and to foster a welcoming attitude among the local population, in the belief that a mutual openness will bring enrichment to all. (EA, no. 65)

CHAPTER II

Reflections in the Light of the Word of God and Catholic Social Teaching

MIGRATION IN THE LIGHT OF THE WORD OF GOD

22. The word of God and the Catholic social teaching it inspires illuminate an understanding—one that is ultimately full of hope—that recognizes the lights and shadows that are a part of the ethical, social, political, economic, and cultural dimensions of migrations between our two countries. The word of God and Catholic social teaching also bring to light the causes that give rise to migrations, as well as the consequences that they have on the communities of origin and destination.

23. These lights and shadows are seen in faith as part of the dynamics of creation and grace on the one hand, and of sin and death on the other, that form the backdrop of all salvation history.

Old Testament

24. Even in the harsh stories of migration, God is present, revealing himself. Abraham stepped out in faith to respond to God's call (Gn 12:1). He and Sarah extended bounteous hospitality to three strangers who were actually a manifestation of the Lord, and this became a paradigm for the response to strangers of Abraham's descendants. The grace of God even broke through situations of sin

in the forced migration of the children of Jacob: Joseph, sold into slavery, eventually became the savior of his family (Gn 37:45)—a type of Jesus, who, betrayed by a friend for thirty pieces of silver, saves the human family.

25. The key events in the history of the Chosen People of enslavement by the Egyptians and of liberation by God led to commandments regarding strangers (Ex 23:9; Lv 19:33). Israel's conduct with the stranger is both an imitation of God and the primary, specific Old Testament manifestation of the great commandment to love one's neighbor: "For the LORD, your God, is the . . . LORD of lords, the great God, mighty and awesome, who has no favorites, accepts no bribes, who executes justice for the orphan and widow, and befriends the alien, feeding and clothing him. So you, too, must befriend the alien, for you were once aliens yourselves in the land of Egypt" (Dt 10:17-19). For the Israelites, these injunctions were not only personal exhortations: the welcome and care of the alien were structured into their gleaning and tithing laws (Lv 19:9-10; Dt 14:28-29).

New Testament

26. Recalling the migration of the Chosen People from Egypt, Jesus, Mary, and Joseph themselves were refugees in Egypt: "Out of Egypt I called my son" (Mt 2:15). From this account the Holy Family has become a figure with whom Christian migrants and refugees throughout the ages can identify, giving them hope and courage in hard times.

St. Matthew also describes the mysterious presence of Jesus in the migrants who frequently lack food and drink and are detained in prison (Mt 25:35-36). The "Son of Man" who "comes in his glory" (Mt 25:31) will judge his followers by the way they respond to those in such need: "Amen, I say to you, whatever you did for one of these least brothers of mine, you did for me" (Mt 25:40).

27. The Risen Christ commanded his apostles to go to all nations to preach his message and to draw all people through faith and baptism into the life of

God the Father, Son, and Holy Spirit (Mt 28:16-20). The Risen Christ sealed this command through the sending of the Holy Spirit (Acts 2:1-21). The triumph of grace in the Resurrection of Christ plants hope in the hearts of all believers, and the Spirit works in the Church to unite all peoples of all races and cultures into the one family of God (Eph 2:17-20).

The Holy Spirit has been present throughout the history of the Church to work against injustice, division, and oppression and to bring about respect for individual human rights, unity of races and cultures, and the incorporation of the marginalized into full life in the Church. In modern times, one of the ways this work of the Spirit has been manifested is through Catholic social teaching, in particular the teachings on human dignity and the principle of solidarity.

MIGRATION IN THE LIGHT OF CATHOLIC SOCIAL TEACHING

28. Catholic teaching has a long and rich tradition in defending the right to migrate. Based on the life and teachings of Jesus, the Church's teaching has provided the basis for the development of basic principles regarding the right to migrate for those attempting to exercise their God-given human rights. Catholic teaching also states that the root causes of migration—poverty, injustice, religious intolerance, armed conflicts—must be addressed so that migrants can remain in their homeland and support their families.

29. In modern times, this teaching has developed extensively in response to the worldwide phenomenon of migration. Pope Pius XII reaffirms the Church's commitment to caring for pilgrims, aliens, exiles, and migrants of every kind in his apostolic constitution *Exsul Familia,* affirming that all peoples have the right to conditions worthy of human life and, if these conditions are not present, the right to migrate. "Then—according to the teachings of [the encyclical] *Rerum Novarum*—the right of the family to a [life worthy of human dignity][6] is recognized. When this happens, migration attains its natural scope as experience often shows."[7]

30. While recognizing the right of the sovereign state to control its borders, *Exsul Familia* also establishes that this right is not absolute, stating that the needs of immigrants must be measured against the needs of the receiving countries:

> Since land everywhere offers the possibility of supporting a large number of people, the sovereignty of the State, although it must be respected, cannot be exaggerated to the point that access to this land is, for inadequate or unjustified reasons, denied to needy and decent people from other nations, provided of course, that the public wealth, considered very carefully, does not forbid this.[8]

In his landmark encyclical *Pacem in Terris*, Blessed Pope John XXIII expands the right to migrate as well as the right to *not* have to migrate: "Every human being has the right to freedom of movement and of residence within the confines of his own country; and, when there are just reasons for it, the right to emigrate to other countries and take up residence there."[9] Pope John XXIII placed limits on immigration, however, when there are "just reasons for it." Nevertheless, he stressed the obligation of sovereign states to promote the universal good where possible, including an obligation to accommodate migration flows. For more powerful nations, a stronger obligation exists.

31. The Church also has recognized the plight of refugees and asylum seekers who flee persecution. In his encyclical letter *Sollicitudo Rei Socialis,* Pope John Paul II refers to the world's refugee crisis as "the festering of a wound."[10] In his 1990 Lenten message, Pope John Paul II lists the rights of refugees, including the right to be reunited with their families and the right to a dignified occupation and just wage. The right to asylum must never be denied when people's lives are truly threatened in their homeland.[11]

32. Pope John Paul II also addresses the more controversial topic of undocumented migration and the undocumented migrant. In his 1995 message for World Migration Day, he notes that such migrants are used by developed nations as a source of labor. Ultimately, the pope says, elimination of global underdevelopment is the antidote to illegal immigration.[12] *Ecclesia in America,* which focuses on the Church in North and South America, reiterates the rights of migrants and their families and the respect for human dignity "even in cases of non-legal immigration."[13]

33. Both of our episcopal conferences have echoed the rich tradition of church teachings with regard to migration.[14] Five principles emerge from such teachings, which guide the Church's view on migration issues.

I. Persons have the right to find opportunities in their homeland.

34. All persons have the right to find in their own countries the economic, political, and social opportunities to live in dignity and achieve a full life through the use of their God-given gifts. In this context, work that provides a just, living wage is a basic human need.

II. Persons have the right to migrate to support themselves and their families.

35. The Church recognizes that all the goods of the earth belong to all people.[15] When persons cannot find employment in their country of origin to support themselves and their families, they have a right to find work elsewhere in order to survive. Sovereign nations should provide ways to accommodate this right.

III. Sovereign nations have the right to control their borders.

36. The Church recognizes the right of sovereign nations to control their territories but rejects such control when it is exerted merely for the purpose of acquiring additional wealth. More powerful economic nations, which have the ability to protect and feed their residents, have a stronger obligation to accommodate migration flows.

IV. Refugees and asylum seekers should be afforded protection.

37. Those who flee wars and persecution should be protected by the global community. This requires, at a minimum, that migrants have a right to claim refugee status without incarceration and to have their claims fully considered by a competent authority.

V. The human dignity and human rights of undocumented migrants should be respected.

38. Regardless of their legal status, migrants, like all persons, possess inherent human dignity that should be respected. Often they are subject to punitive laws and harsh treatment from enforcement officers from both receiving and transit countries. Government policies that respect the basic human rights of the undocumented are necessary.

39. The Church recognizes the right of a sovereign state to control its borders in furtherance of the common good. It also recognizes the right of human persons to migrate so that they can realize their God-given rights. These teachings complement each other. While the sovereign state may impose reasonable limits on immigration, the common good is not served when the basic human rights of the individual are violated. In the current condition of the world, in which global poverty and persecution are rampant, the presumption is that persons must migrate in order to support and protect themselves and that nations who are able to receive them should do so whenever possible. It is through this lens that we assess the current migration reality between the United States and Mexico.

CHAPTER III

Pastoral Challenges and Responses

TOWARD CONVERSION

40. Our concern as pastors for the dignity and rights of migrants extends to pastoral responses as well as public policy issues. The Church in our two countries is constantly challenged to see the face of Christ, crucified and risen, in the stranger. The whole Church is challenged to live the experience of the disciples on the road to Emmaus (Lk 24:13-25), as they are converted to be witnesses of the Risen Lord after they welcome him as a stranger. Faith in the presence of Christ in the migrant leads to a conversion of mind and heart, which leads to a renewed spirit of communion and to the building of structures of solidarity to accompany the migrant. Part of the process of conversion of mind and heart deals with confronting attitudes of cultural superiority, indifference, and racism; accepting migrants not as foreboding aliens, terrorists, or economic threats, but rather as persons with dignity and rights, revealing the presence of Christ; and recognizing migrants as bearers of deep cultural values and rich faith traditions. Church leaders at every level are called on to communicate this teaching as well as to provide instruction on the phenomenon of migration, its causes, and its impact throughout the world. This instruction should be grounded in the Scriptures and social teaching.

TOWARD COMMUNION

41. Conversion of mind and heart leads to communion expressed through hospitality on the part of receiving communities and a sense of belonging and welcome on the part of those in the communities where migrants are arriving.

The New Testament often counsels that hospitality is a virtue necessary for all followers of Jesus. Many migrants, sensing rejection or indifference from Catholic communities, have sought solace outside the Church. They experience the sad fate of Jesus, recorded in St. John's Gospel: "He came to what was his own, but his own people did not accept him" (Jn 1:11). The need to provide hospitality and create a sense of belonging pertains to the Church on every level, as Pope John Paul II said in his annual message on World Migration Day 1993: "The families of migrants . . . should be able to find a homeland everywhere in the Church."[16]

42. We bishops have the primary responsibility to build up the spirit of hospitality and communion extended to migrants who are passing through or to immigrants who are settling in the area.

- We call upon pastors and lay leaders to ensure support for migrant and immigrant families.
- We urge communities to offer migrant families hospitality, not hostility, along their journey.
- We commend church communities that have established migrant shelters that provide appropriate pastoral and social services to migrants.
- We encourage Catholics and all people of good will to work with the community to address the causes of undocumented migration and to protect the human rights of all migrants.
- We call on the local church to help newcomers integrate in ways that are respectful, that celebrate their cultures, and that are responsive to their social needs, leading to a mutual enrichment of the local church.
- We ask that special attention be given to migrant and immigrant children and youth as they straddle two cultures, especially to give them opportunities for leadership and service in the community and to encourage vocations among them.

- The Church on both sides of the border must dedicate resources to provide pastoral care for migrants who are detained or incarcerated. The presence of the Church within detention facilities and jails is an essential way of addressing the human rights violations that migrants may face when they are apprehended.
- We encourage local dioceses to sponsor pertinent social services for migrants and immigrants, particularly affordable legal services.
- In many rural dioceses, the primary site of pastoral outreach for farm workers is the migrant camp, usually at a significant distance from the parish church. In this context we encourage local parishioners to be prepared as home missionaries and the migrants themselves to be prepared as catechists and outreach workers.

TOWARD SOLIDARITY

43. The building of community with migrants and new immigrants leads to a growing sense of solidarity. The bishop as pastor of the local church should lead the priests, deacons, religious, and faithful in promoting justice and in denouncing injustice towards migrants and immigrants, courageously defending their basic human rights. This should be true in both the sending and receiving churches. As leaven in the society, pastoral agents can be instruments for peace and justice to promote systemic change by making legislators and other government officials aware of what they see in the community. Working closely with other advocates for workers and with non-governmental organizations, the Church can be instrumental in developing initiatives for social change that benefit the most vulnerable members of the community.

44. The Church should encourage these broad-based efforts to provide both a comprehensive network of social services and advocacy for migrant families. Another important resource these communities can offer migrants, especially those seeking asylum or family reunification, is affordable or free legal assistance. A special call is issued to lawyers in both our countries to assist individuals and families in navigating the arduous immigration process and to defend the human rights of migrants, especially those in detention. Parishes should work together to provide adequate services throughout the community, making every effort to invite parishioners with special expertise (lawyers, doctors, social workers) to assist generously wherever they can.

PASTORAL CARE AT ORIGIN, IN TRANSIT, AND AT DESTINATIONS

45. The reality of migration, especially when the journey entails clandestine border crossings, is often fraught with uncertainties and even dangers. As migrants leave their homes, pastoral counseling should be offered to help them to better understand these realities and to consider alternative options, including the exploration of available legal means of immigration.

Native Peoples Deserve Special Consideration

The one ancestral homeland of the Tohono O'odham nation that stretches across the United States and Mexico has no border. Neither does the homeland of the Yaqui nation. Tribal members' rights to travel freely throughout the land they have inhabited for one thousand years should be respected. They should be able to visit family members and participate in religious and cultural celebrations, observances, and other community events without harassment or multiple identity checks in both Mexico and the United States.

46. Prayer books and guides to social and religious services should be provided along the way and at the points of arrival. The migrants should be reminded of their role as evangelizers: that they have the capacity to evangelize others by the daily witness of their Christian lives. Special encouragement should be given to migrants to be faithful to their spouses and families and to thereby live out the sacrament of marriage. Support of the family that is left behind is also needed. Migration under certain conditions can have a devastating effect on families; at times, entire villages are depopulated of their young people.

47. Dioceses in Mexico and the United States need to work closely to provide a sacramental presence for migrants. Ideally, local parishes should ensure that sacramental preparation is available to people on the move, making special provisions for them given their transitory lives of following work wherever it leads. Eucharistic celebrations or communion services and the Sacrament of Reconciliation should be available to migrants where they can easily attend, and at times that best suit working people with families.

COLLABORATIVE PASTORAL RESPONSES

48. *Ecclesia in America* recommends collaboration between episcopal conferences for more effective pastoral responses. Collaboration is most needed in the development of a more systematic approach to ministerial accompaniment of migrants. The numbers of migrants who leave Central and South America and Mexico and who enter the United States are so large that a more concerted effort is needed in the preparation of priests, religious, and lay leaders who accompany them.

49. In previous centuries, when immigrants from eastern and western Europe came to all parts of the American continent, the Church in some countries established national seminaries to prepare priests to serve in the lands where others in their country were settling, particularly in North and South America. In other countries, the Church developed religious communities of men and women to accompany emigrants on their way, to minister to them on arrival, and to help them integrate into their new homes from a position of strength, often by forming national or personal parishes. In still other countries, the Church has developed exchange or temporary programs in which commitments are made to supply priests for a period of three to five years. Up to the present there have been individual exchanges of priests between Central and South American, Mexican, and U.S. dioceses. The bishops from Central and South America and Mexico have visited the U.S. dioceses to which these priests and their people have immigrated, and U.S. bishops have visited dioceses in Central and South America and Mexico, reflecting the teaching of the Second Vatican Council that every local church is missionary, both as sending and receiving church. This exchange has built up the spirit of collaboration encouraged in *Ecclesia in America.* These efforts have been very positive, but the results have not been uniform.

50. Careful and generous cooperation between dioceses is important to provide priests and religious who are suited for this important ministry. Guidelines for their training and reception by the host diocese must be developed jointly with the diocese that sends them. During their stay in the host diocese, international priests and religious deserve an extensive and careful orientation and gracious welcome. As immigrants themselves, they too experience the loss of a familiar and supportive environment and must have the support they need to adjust to the new environment and culture. Periodically, as resources allow, they should be encouraged to return to their home dioceses or motherhouses to rest and to reconnect with their communities.

51. A next step would be to study the possibility of a more comprehensive preparation and assignment of clergy, religious, and lay people who dedicate themselves to pastoral accompaniment of migrants. Such a study by representatives of both episcopal conferences should focus on the following:

- The needs of migrants on their journey and at the points of their arrival
- The dioceses most in need of priests, religious, and lay leaders
- The possibility of seminaries in Mexico to prepare priests for service in the United States
- The assignment of religious communities to accompany migrants

The study also should include recommendations on ways to build bridges of exchange between dioceses and on effective programs to orient ministers to the new culture they will enter. This formation should be an integral process of human development, educational enrichment, language acquisition, intercultural communication, and spiritual formation. In order to meet this critical need as soon as possible, cooperation with existing seminaries, schools of theology, and pastoral institutes is highly encouraged.

This study should also investigate ways to help the immigrants themselves to continue an active role as lay leaders in the new settings in which they find themselves and ways for the receiving church to animate and encourage them, especially those who served as catechists and community leaders in the country of origin. We recommend that a special academic subject on pastoral migration or human mobility be included as part of the regular curriculum in our seminaries, institutions, and houses of formation.

52. Another area of collaboration could be in the preparation of catechetical materials that would be culturally appropriate for migrant farm workers. Several examples already exist that reflect the collaboration of dioceses along both the United States–Mexico border and the Mexico–Guatemala border.

53. This cross-border collaboration has already reaped positive results, such as the development of legal services, social services, cooperation with houses of hospitality along the borders, and prayer books for the journey. Joint prayer services at the border, such as the *Posadas*, Good Friday vigils, and All Souls rites to cherish the memory of those who have died, also have been held.

54. To develop and continue the cooperation between the Church in the United States and Mexico, we bishops encourage ongoing dialogue between bishops and pastoral workers on the border, exchanges between dioceses, and continuing meetings between the USCCB's Committee on Migration and the CEM's Episcopal Commission for the Pastoral Care for People on the Move.

55. *Ecclesia in America* summed up these pastoral recommendations as follows:

> Migrants should be met with a hospitable and welcoming attitude which can encourage them to become part of the Church's life, always with due regard for their freedom and their specific cultural identity. Cooperation between the dioceses from which they come and those in which they settle, also through specific pastoral structures provided for in the legislation and praxis of the Church, has proved extremely beneficial to this end. In this way the most adequate and complete pastoral care possible can be ensured. The Church in America must be constantly concerned to provide for the effective evangelization of those recent arrivals who do not yet know Christ. (no. 65)

MEXICO
NADA QUE DECLARAR
NOTHING TO DECLARE
NADA QUE DECLARAR
NOTHING TO DECLARE
NADA QUE DECLARAR
NOTHING TO DECLARE
NADA QUE DECLARAR
NOTHING TO DECLARE
ALTO
STOP
ALTO
STOP

CHAPTER IV

Public Policy Challenges and Responses

56. The United States and Mexico share a special relationship that requires focused attention upon joint concerns. The realities of migration between both nations require comprehensive policy responses implemented in unison by both countries. The current relationship is weakened by inconsistent and divergent policies that are not coordinated and, in many cases, address only the *symptoms* of the migration phenomenon and not its root *causes*.

57. Now is the time for both the United States and Mexico to confront the reality of globalization and to work toward a globalization of solidarity. We call upon both governments to cooperate and to jointly enact policies that will create a generous, legal flow of migrants between both nations. Both governments have recognized the integration of economic interests through the North American Free Trade Agreement (NAFTA). It is now time to harmonize policies on the movement of people, particularly in a way that respects the human dignity of the migrant and recognizes the social consequences of globalization.

58. With these goals in mind, we offer several policy recommendations for both nations to consider that address the root causes of migration, legal avenues for migration, and humane law enforcement. These recommendations focus upon both U.S. and Mexican government policies toward newcomers in their own nations, since both are receiving countries.

ADDRESSING THE ROOT CAUSES OF MIGRATION

59. As we have stated, persons should have the opportunity to remain in their homeland to support and to find full lives for themselves and their families. This is the ideal situation for which the world and both countries must strive: one in which migration flows are driven by choice, not necessity. Paramount to achieving this goal is the need to develop the economies of sending nations, including Mexico.

60. Only a long-term effort that adjusts economic inequalities between the United States and Mexico will provide Mexican workers with employment opportunities that will allow them to remain at home and to support themselves and their families. The Church has consistently singled out economic inequality between nations as a global disorder that must be addressed. Within the United States–Mexico relationship, we have witnessed the application of economic policies that do not adequately take into account the welfare of individual proprietors who struggle to survive. For example, the North America Free Trade Agreement (NAFTA) has harmed small businesses in Mexico, especially in the rural sector. Both nations should reconsider the impact of economic a nd trade agreements on persons who work hard at making a living through individual enterprises.

61. The creation of employment opportunities in Mexico would help to reduce poverty and would mitigate the incentive for many migrants to look for employment in the United States. The implementation of economic policies in Mexico that create living-wage jobs is vital, especially for Mexican citizens without advanced skills. Targeted development projects in Mexican municipalities and rural areas that traditionally have had the highest rates of emigration are necessary. Projects and resources particularly should be targeted to the Mexican agricultural sector and small businesses.

62. As border regions are the focal point of the migration phenomenon, resources also should be directed toward communities on the United States–Mexico border. Such additional resources would augment existing efforts by border residents to aid migrants in meeting their most basic needs. We urge the initiation of joint border development projects that would help build up the economies of these areas so that border residents may continue to work and live cooperatively. Church leaders should work with both communities on the U.S. and Mexican border and both communities on the Mexican and Guatemalan border to help them to overcome fears and prejudices.

CREATING LEGAL AVENUES FOR MIGRATION

63. With both the United States and Mexico experiencing economic, social, and cultural integration on an unprecedented scale, it is important that both governments formally acknowledge this reality by enacting reforms in the immigration systems of both countries.

Family-Based Immigration

64. As pastors, we are troubled by how the current amalgamation of immigration laws, policies, and actions pursued by both governments often impedes family unity. While the majority of Mexican migrants enter the United States to find work, many cross the border to join family members.

65. The U.S. legal immigration system places per-country limits on visas for family members of U.S. legal permanent residents from Mexico. This cap, along with processing delays, has resulted in unacceptable waiting times for the legal reunification of a husband and wife, or of a parent and child. For example, the spouse or child of a Mexican-born legal permanent resident can wait approximately eight years to obtain a visa to join loved ones in the United States. Spouses and parents thus face a difficult decision: either honor their moral

commitment to family and migrate to the United States without proper documentation, or wait in the system and face indefinite separation from loved ones.

66. This is an unacceptable choice, and a policy that *encourages* undocumented migration. In order to ensure that families remain together, reform of the U.S. family-based legal immigration categories vis-à-vis Mexico is necessary. A new framework must be established that will give Mexican families more opportunities to legally reunite with their loved ones in the United States.[17] This would help alleviate the long waiting times and, in time, would *reduce* undocumented migration between the United States and Mexico.

67. Family unity also is weakened when the children of immigrants are left unprotected. In the United States, birthright citizenship should be maintained as an important principle in U.S. immigration law. In Mexico, some children are being denied birth certificates and consequent Mexican nationality due to their parents' undocumented status. As the Mexican Constitution ensures and Article 68 of the National Law of Population codifies, such children have the right and protection to be documented at birth. Otherwise, their access to health, education, and other basic services may be denied later in life. Moreover, the right to an identity and nationality are enshrined in international covenants.

Legalization of the Undocumented

68. Approximately 10.5 million Mexican-born persons currently live in the United States, about 5.5 million of whom reside legally, and the remainder of whom have undocumented status. Each year, an estimated 150,000 Mexican migrants enter the United States without authorization, working in such industries as agriculture, service, entertainment, and construction.[18] Despite the rhetoric from anti-immigrant groups and some government officials, they labor with the quiet acquiescence of both government and industry.

69. A broad legalization program of the undocumented would benefit not only the migrants but also both nations. Making legal the large number of undocumented workers from many nations who are in the United States would help to stabilize the labor market in the United States, to preserve family unity, and to improve the standard of living in immigrant communities. Moreover, migrant workers, many of whom have established roots in their communities, will continue to contribute to the U.S. economy.

70. Legalization also would maintain the flow of remittances to Mexico and would give Mexicans safe and legal passage back to Mexico, if necessary. In addition, such legalization would promote national security by reducing fear in immigrant communities and by encouraging undocumented persons to become participating members of society. Legalization represents sound public policy and should be featured in any migration agreement between the United States and Mexico. In order to ensure fairness for all nationalities, the U.S. Congress should enact a legalization program for immigrants regardless of their country of origin.

71. In the case of Mexico, the legalization programs that the Mexican National Migration Institute have executed provide a good beginning. The benefits of legalization have been evident to the migrants themselves, since they may now work with the protection of their basic labor rights; and to the government, which can now gain a more realistic picture of the population present in the country. We hope that future programs will provide more publicity and information to the public, will increase the number of and better train those who administer them, and will decrease the cost to the applicant, which in the past has disadvantaged those with lesser means.[19]

Employment-Based Immigration

72. In the context of the United States–Mexico bilateral relationship, the United States needs Mexican laborers to maintain a healthy economy and should make a special effort to provide legal avenues for Mexican workers to obtain in the United States jobs that provide a living wage and appropriate benefits and labor protections. The U.S. employment-based immigration system should be reformed to feature both *permanent* and, with appropriate protections, *temporary* visa programs for laborers. A system that is transparent and that protects the rights of workers should be formulated. Visa costs of the program should remain affordable for all who wish to participate. Reform in worker programs must be coupled with a broad-based legalization program.

Remittances: The Lifeblood of Many Mexican Families

Mexican workers who labor in the United States send large portions of their wages, which they have earned by the sweat of their brows, back to their families in Mexico. Termed "remittances," these funds amount to as much as $8-10 billion a year, representing one of the largest sources of foreign currency in Mexico. These funds are an important source of support for many families in Mexico. Unfortunately, many Mexican workers in the United States must pay exorbitant fees (some as high as 20 percent) to send remittances to their families in Mexico. Perhaps a more efficient means can be devised for sending funds to Mexico that would result in more of the money reaching those in need. Furthermore, arrangements could be made with the organizations that process these remittances to channel some of their earnings from the fees to support community development efforts in Mexico, such as road construction, sewers, health clinics, and so on. Such an approach could be further expanded by making arrangements with the U.S. and Mexican governments to match developmental funds paid through fee revenues in order to augment the investment in sustainable community development programs.

73. A certain number of work visas should be created to allow laborers to enter the country as legal permanent residents. Family ties and work history in the United States are two of the possible factors that should be considered in allocating such visas. A visa category featuring permanent residency would recognize the contributions of long-term laborers and would ensure that their labor rights are respected.

74. More problematic is the reform of U.S. temporary worker programs. The first U.S. agricultural temporary-worker program, known as the *Bracero* program, ended abruptly in 1964 because of widespread evidence of corruption and abuse of workers. The current program, which allows more than thirty thousand workers to enter the United States each year, is marked by a lack of enforcement of worker protections and by insufficient wages and benefits to support a family.

75. Nevertheless, we recognize that, as an alternative to undocumented migration, an efficient legal pathway must be established that protects the basic labor rights of foreign-born workers. In order to prevent future abuse of workers, any new temporary worker program must afford Mexican and other foreign workers wage levels and employment benefits that are sufficient to support a family in dignity; must include worker protections and job portability that U.S. workers have; must allow for family unity; must employ labor-market tests to ensure that U.S. workers are protected; and must grant workers the ability to move easily and securely between the United States and their homelands. It must employ strong enforcement mechanisms to protect workers' rights and give workers the option to become lawful permanent residents after a specific amount of time. In addition, the United States and Mexico should conclude a Social Security agreement that allows workers to accrue benefits for work performed during participation in the program.

76. A properly constructed worker program would reduce the number of undocumented persons migrating from Mexico to the United States, lessening the calls for border enforcement and the demand for the services of unscrupulous smugglers.

77. Moreover, in order to honor the labor rights of foreign-born workers, the United States should sign the International Convention on the Protection of the Rights of All Migrant Workers and Members of Their Families, which lays out principles for the protection of the labor and human rights of migrant workers.[20] Mexico, already a signatory, should implement its principles without current reservations.

HUMANE ENFORCEMENT POLICIES IN MEXICO AND THE UNITED STATES

Enforcement Tactics

78. As explained above, the Catholic Church recognizes the right and responsibility of sovereign nations to control their borders and to ensure the security interests of their citizens. Therefore, we accept the legitimate role of the U.S. and Mexican governments in intercepting undocumented migrants who attempt to travel through or cross into one of the two countries. We do not accept, however, some of the policies and tactics that our governments have employed to meet this shared responsibility.

79. The men and women of the law enforcement agencies charged with maintaining the United States–Mexico border have difficult jobs that require long hours in sometimes extreme conditions. Unfortunately, the enforcement policies that they implement have had the effect of undermining the human dignity of migrants and creating a confrontational and violent relationship between enforcement officers and migrants. Steps must be taken to create an environment in which force is used only in the most necessary circumstances,

U.S. Enforcement Strategy Fails to Deter Migrants

In 1994, the U.S. government adopted a new border enforcement strategy designed to deter migrants from entering the United States from Mexico. The Immigration and Naturalization Service (INS) has launched several blockade initiatives over the past several years, including "Operation Hold the Line," in El Paso, Texas, in 1993; "Operation Gatekeeper," in the San Diego, California, region in 1994; and "Operation Safeguard," in southern Arizona, in 1995. According to an August 2001 report by the U.S. General Accounting Office (GAO), the primary discernible effect of the enforcement strategy has been to divert migrants away from the largest concentration of enforcement resources, most typically to remote regions of the southwestern United States. During the same period, the number of undocumented persons in the United States has more than doubled, from four million in 1994 to more than eight million in 2000.

and only to the extent needed, to protect the physical well-being of both the enforcement officer and the migrant. This requires not only a review and reform of enforcement tactics, but also, more importantly, a reshaping of the enforcement policies of both nations.

80. Alarmingly, migrants often are treated as criminals by civil enforcement authorities. Misperceptions and xenophobic and racist attitudes in both the United States and Mexico contribute to an atmosphere in which undocumented persons are discriminated against and abused. Reports of physical abuse of migrants by U.S. Border Patrol agents, the Mexican authorities, and in some cases, U.S. and Mexican residents are all too frequent, including the use of excessive force and the shackling of migrants' hands and feet.

81. In the United States, documented abuses of migrants occur frequently. To be sure, the large majority of Border Patrol agents conduct themselves in a professional and respectful manner. But there exist those who perpetrate abuses and who are not held accountable by the U.S. government.[21]

82. In addition, the U.S. record of handling undocumented unaccompanied minors from Mexico and other countries is shameful. Mexican children intercepted along the U.S. border often are placed in dilapidated detention facilities for days at a time until they can be repatriated. Children from Mexico and other countries in Central America often are not given the option to contact an attorney, guardian, or relative, or to file for asylum. These practices must stop. Because of their heightened vulnerability, unaccompanied minors require special consideration and care.

83. Mexican enforcement of immigration laws, targeted specifically through racial profiling of migrants attempting to reach the United States, has been marked by corruption, police brutality, and systemic abuses of basic human rights. Migrants often are forced to bribe Mexican police to continue transit and, if unable to produce payments, are beaten and returned to the border. Because of the lack of rights and policies that drive undocumented migrants away from small urban areas, the migrants often are assaulted by bandits in the border area between Ciudad Hidalgo, Mexico, and Tecun Uman, Guatemala. We know of migrants from Central America who pay thousands of dollars to smugglers to shepherd them through Mexico but who, in some cases, are kidnapped. Their families never hear from them again.

84. Although we acknowledge that the government of Mexico has improved the administration of the migration system and is attempting to bring the rule of law to it, Mexican immigration policies remain unclear and inconsistent. Corruption continues to weaken the Mexican migration system and to hurt the common good. We urge the Mexican National Migration Institute to

strengthen the participation of civil society organizations in its Delegation Councils[22] as partners to bring healthy transparency to the country's migration system.

85. In order to address these excesses, both governments must create training mechanisms that instruct enforcement agents in the use of appropriate tactics for enforcing immigration law. We urge the U.S. and Mexican governments to include human rights curricula in their training regimens so that immigration enforcement personnel are more sensitive to the handling of undocumented migrants.[23] Community organizations, including dioceses and parishes, can assist enforcement officials in this effort. In addition, the enforcement function in both nations should be left to federal authorities (the Immigration and Naturalization Service and Border Patrol in the United States, and the National Migration Institute and Federal Preventive Police in Mexico), not transferred to local police who necessarily have other priorities and who are untrained in the proper methods for enforcing immigration law. Military personnel from any branch or service should not be used to enforce migration laws along either country's land borders.

Border Enforcement Policies

86. Of particular concern are the border enforcement policies pursued by both governments that have contributed to the abuse and even deaths of migrants in both Mexico and the United States. Along the United States–Mexico border, the U.S. government has launched several border-blockade initiatives in the past decade designed to discourage undocumented migrants from entering the country. These initiatives have been characterized by a tripling of Border Patrol agents, especially at ports of entry, and the use of sophisticated technology such as ground sensors, surveillance cameras, heat-detecting scopes, and reinforced fencing.

87. Rather than significantly reducing illegal crossings, the initiatives have instead driven migrants into remote and dangerous areas of the southwest region of the United States, leading to an alarming number of migrant deaths.

Since the beginning of 1998, official statistics indicate that more than two thousand migrants have lost their lives trying to cross the United States–Mexico border, many from environmental causes such as heat stroke, dehydration, hypothermia, or drowning. The blockades also have contributed to an increase in migrant smuggling, in which desperate migrants pay high fees to smugglers to get them into the United States. In recent years, smuggling has become a more organized and profitable enterprise.[24]

"Come and Look at My Brother in His Coffin"

Jose Luis Hernandez Aguirre tried desperately to find work in the *maquiladora* plants near Mexicali but was unable to do so. With a wife and two children, ages one and seven, Jose needed to find a job that would put food on the table. A smuggler told him of the high-paying jobs across the border and offered, for $1,000, to take him there. Joined by his brother Jaime and several others, the group headed for the United States with hope. After one day, brother Jaime called and reported to the family and Jose's sister, Sonia, that Jose was lost. Jaime could not make the trek in the desert, but Jose wanted to continue on the journey. He had to find a job for his family. Four days later, Jose's body was found in the desert. His sister Sonia borrowed a truck to retrieve Jose's remains. Upon her return, she encountered another group of migrants heading to the United States. "Why do you want to risk your lives like this?" she implored. "Come and look at my brother in his coffin."

88. In southern Mexico, similar policies have resulted in countless migrant deaths along the Suchiate River, most by drowning. Another cause for concern is the presence of Mexican checkpoints—far from most urban areas and difficult to monitor for human rights abuses—which are manned by military and federal, state, and local police agencies along the country's borders and interior. Because

these checkpoints are used as "choke" points for arms, drugs, and migrant smuggling, there is an unfair tendency to associate migrants with criminal activity.

89. We urge both the U.S. and Mexican enforcement authorities to abandon the type of strategies that give rise to migrant smuggling operations and migrant deaths. Care should be taken not to push migrants to routes in which their lives may be in danger. The U.S. Border Patrol has recently launched a border safety initiative to prevent migrant deaths. We ask the Border Patrol to redouble their efforts in this area and to work more closely with community groups to identify and rescue migrants in distress. We also urge more concerted efforts to root out smuggling enterprises at their source using a wide range of intelligence and investigative tactics. In other church documents, the U.S. bishops have also expressed concern about the increasing drug-trafficking industry.[25]

90. Similarly, we call upon both nations to undertake joint efforts to halt the scourge of trafficking in human persons, both within our hemisphere and internationally. Trafficking in persons—in which men, women, and children from all over the globe are transported to other countries for the purposes of forced prostitution or labor—inherently rejects the dignity of the human person and exploits conditions of global poverty.

91. Both governments must vigilantly seek to end trafficking in human persons. The U.S. government should vigorously enforce recent laws that target traffickers both at home and abroad. Mexican authorities must strengthen efforts to identify and to destroy trafficking operations within Mexico. Together, both governments should more effectively share information on trafficking operations and should engage in joint action to apprehend and prosecute traffickers.

Due Process Rights

92. In 1996, the U.S. Congress eviscerated due process rights for migrants with the passage of the Illegal Immigration Reform and Immigrant Responsibility Act (IIRIRA), which authorizes the detention and deportation of migrants for relatively minor offenses, even after they have served their sentences. IIRIRA has caused the unjust separation of untold numbers of immigrant families.[26] We urge the U.S. Congress to revisit this law and to make appropriate changes consistent with due process rights.

93. We also urge the Mexican government to honor the right to due process for all those who are in the country, specifically documented and undocumented migrants who do not now enjoy due process and who may be removed from the country for arbitrary reasons. Recognizing such a right only strengthens the rule of law in a country and further legitimates its institutions.[27]

94. Once apprehended, migrants often are held in unsanitary and crowded prisons, jails, and detention centers, in Mexico and the United States, sometimes alongside serious criminal offenders. Migrants without documentation should not be treated as criminals, should be detained for the least amount of time possible, and should have access to the necessary medical, legal, and spiritual services. Asylum seekers who pass an initial "credible fear" interview should be released.

Protecting Human Rights in Regional Migration Policies

95. As defenders of those who flee persecution in foreign lands, we are increasingly troubled by the asylum policies employed by both the United States and Mexico. Most alarming is the prospect of creating a North American exterior boundary system in which asylum policies would be regionalized in such a way as to deny asylum seekers appropriate judicial remedies and protection.[28]

96. Increasingly, asylum seekers from across the globe are smuggled through Central America to Mexico and the United States. They come from as far away as China, India, Iran, and Iraq. In most cases, they have valid claims for protection, but many are swept up in anti-smuggling initiatives in Central America and Mexico and are sent back to their persecutors without proper screening.

97. The denial of asylum adjudication rights is an especially acute problem along the United States–Mexico border. Employing a U.S. policy known as *expedited removal*, U.S. immigration officers routinely detain and deport migrants without giving them a hearing before an immigration judge. In fact, expedited removal is most heavily used against Mexicans. Of the just over 180,000 total removals from the United States in FY1999 and FY2000, 81 percent of those deported were Mexican.[29] Moreover, Mexicans and others deported under expedited removal are subject to being barred from readmission to the United States

for at least five years. Along the southern border of Mexico, migrants are returned on a regular basis to Central America without screening.

98. Denying access to asylum procedures, making them complicated, or not providing clear information about them in languages that people can understand is a grave injustice and violates the spirit of international law and commitments made by both our countries.[30]

99. We restate our long-held position that asylum seekers and refugees should have access to qualified adjudicators who will objectively consider their pleas. We urge both countries to take a leadership role in the Regional Conference on Migration (*Puebla* Process) and to work with our Central American neighbors to ensure that asylum seekers and refugees throughout our hemisphere have access to appropriate due process protections consistent with international law.

CONSEQUENCES OF SEPTEMBER 11 TERRORIST ATTACKS FOR MIGRANTS

100. The terrorist attacks of September 11, 2001, which ended so tragically in New York, the Washington, D.C., area, and Pennsylvania, have placed national security concerns at the forefront of the migration debate and have added another dimension to the migration relationship between the United States and Mexico. Certain security actions are a necessary response to credible terrorist threats, such as improved intelligence sharing and screening, enhanced visa and passport security, and thorough checks at the United States–Mexico border. Other actions, however, such as reducing legal immigration between the two nations, do not serve to make the United States or Mexico more secure. We urge both nations to cooperate in this area, but not to enact joint policies that undermine human rights, reduce legal immigration, or deny asylum seekers opportunities for protection.

Conclusion

101. As bishops we have decided, in the words of Pope John Paul II, to "put out into the deep"[31] in search of common initiatives that will promote solidarity between our countries, particularly among the Catholics of both countries. We are committed to the new evangelization of our continent and to the search for new ways of leading our peoples to encounter Christ, who is "the path to conversion, communion and solidarity" (EA, no. 7).[32]

102. We recognize the phenomenon of migration as an authentic sign of the times. We see it in both our countries through the suffering of those who have been forced to become migrants for many reasons. To such a sign we must respond in common and creative ways so that we may strengthen the faith, hope, and charity of migrants and all the People of God. Such a sign is a call to transform national and international social, economic, and political structures so that they may provide the conditions required for the development for all, without exclusion and discrimination against any person in any circumstance.

103. In effect, the Church is increasingly called to be "sign and instrument both of a very closely knit union with God and of the unity of the whole human race" (*Lumen Gentium*, no. 1). The Catholic bishops of the United States and Mexico, in communion with the Holy Father in his 1995 World Migration Day message, affirm that

> In the Church no one is a stranger, and the Church is not foreign to anyone, anywhere. As a sacrament of unity and thus a sign and a binding force for the whole human race, the Church is the place where illegal immigrants are also recognized and accepted as brothers and sisters. It is the

> task of the various Dioceses actively to ensure that these people, who are obliged to live outside the safety net of civil society, may find a sense of brotherhood in the Christian community. Solidarity means taking responsibility for those in trouble.

The Church must, therefore, welcome all persons regardless of race, culture, language, and nation with joy, charity, and hope. It must do so with special care for those who find themselves—regardless of motive—in situations of poverty, marginalization, and exclusion.

104. We ask our presidents to continue negotiations on migration issues to achieve a system of migration between the two countries that is more generous, just, and humane. We call for legislatures of our two countries to effect a conscientious revision of the immigration laws and to establish a binational system that accepts migration flows, guaranteeing the dignity and human rights of the migrant. We ask public officials who are in charge of formulating, implementing, and executing immigration laws to reexamine national and local policies toward the migrant and to use their leadership positions to erase misconceptions about migration. We ask adjudicators who process immigrants' legal claims to create a welcoming atmosphere that does not threaten their confidence or security. We encourage the media to support and promote a genuine attitude of welcoming toward migrants and immigrants.

105. We, the Catholic bishops of the United States and Mexico, pledge ourselves to defend the migrant. We also pledge to support the creation of the necessary conditions so that all may enjoy the fruit of their work and life in their homeland, if they so wish.

106. We stand in solidarity with you, our migrant brothers and sisters, and we will continue to advocate on your behalf for just and fair migration policies. We commit ourselves to animate communities of Christ's disciples on both sides of the border to accompany you on your journey so that yours will truly be a journey of hope, not of despair, and so that, at the point of arrival, you will experience that you are strangers no longer and instead members of God's household. We pray that, wherever you go, you will always be conscious of your dignity as human beings and of your call to bring the Good News of Jesus Christ, who came that we "might have life and have it more abundantly" (Jn 10:10). We invite you who are forced to emigrate to maintain contact with your homes and, especially, to maintain fidelity to your families so that you treasure your cultural values and the gift of faith and so that you bring these treasures to whatever place you go.

107. The appearance of Our Lady of Guadalupe to St. Juan Diego revealed the compassionate presence of God reaching out to Mary to be in solidarity with and to give hope to a suffering people. In the same spirit, we, the Catholic bishops of the United States of Mexico and the United States of America, have written this letter to give hope to suffering migrants. We pray that you will experience the same hope that inspired St. Paul in his Letter to the Romans:

> What will separate us from the love of Christ? Will anguish, or distress, or persecution, or famine, or nakedness, or peril, or the sword? As it is written: "For your sake we are being slain all the day; we are looked upon as sheep to be slaughtered." No, in all these things we conquer overwhelmingly through Him who loved us. For I am convinced that neither death, nor life, nor angels, nor principalities, nor present things, nor future things, nor powers, nor height, nor depth, nor any other creature will be able to separate us from the love of God in Christ Jesus our Lord. (Rom 8:35-39)

108. And may the blessing of Almighty God come down upon you and be with you forever: the blessing of God the Father, who loves you with an everlasting love, the blessing of God the Son, who was called out of exile in Egypt to be our Savior, and the blessing of God the Holy Spirit, who guides you to extend Christ's reign wherever you go. And may Mary of Guadalupe, our mother, bring you safely home.

Delivered on the fourth anniversary of Ecclesia in America, *January 22, 2003, Washington, D.C., U.S.A., and Mexico City, Mexico.*

Appendix: Definitions

Asylee: See *Refugee,* below. The definition conforms to that of a refugee except regarding the location of the person upon application for asylum: The asylee applies for protection in the country of asylum, whereas the refugee applies for status in either his or her home country (under certain circumstances) or in a country of temporary asylum.

Globalization: The process whereby the world's goods, communications, and peoples are more fully integrated, accessible, and interdependent.

Immigrant: A person who moves to another country to take up permanent residence.

Legal Immigrant: A person who has been admitted to reside and work on a permanent basis in the United States; admission is most commonly based on reunification with close family members or employment.

Migrant: A person on the move, either voluntarily or involuntarily, in the person's own country, internationally, or both. Unlike refugees, migrants are commonly considered free to return home whenever they wish because their lives are not in danger there.

Refugee: Any person, who, owing to a well-founded fear of being persecuted for reasons of race, religion, nationality, membership in a particular social group, or political opinion, is outside the country of his or her nationality and is unable or, owing to such fear, is unwilling, to avail himself or herself of the protection of that country; or who, not having a nationality and being outside the country of his or her habitual residence as a result of such events, is unable or, owing to such fear, is unwilling to return to it (source: United Nations International Law).

Undocumented immigrant: A person who is in a country without the permission of that country's government. Such persons are called "undocumented" because they lack the required paperwork.

Notes

1 The synod was held in Vatican City from November 16 to December 12, 1997.

2 Cf. Conferencia del Episcopado Mexicano (CEM), *Del Encuentro con Jesucristo a la Solidaridad con Todos* (México, DF: CEM, 2000). United States Conference of Catholic Bishops (USCCB), *Welcoming the Stranger Among Us: Unity in Diversity* (Washington, D.C.: USCCB, 2000).

3 Melissa Therrien and Roberto R. Ramirez, *The Hispanic Population in the United States: March 2000*, Current Population Report P20-535 (Washington, D.C.: U.S. Census Bureau, 2000).

4 Immigration and Naturalization Service, press release "INS Announces Legal Immigration Figures for FY2001," Washington, D.C., August 30, 2002.

5 V. Maccagnan, ed. Stefano de Fiores and Salvatore Meo, "*Guadalupe*," *Nuevo Diccionario de Mariologia* (Madrid: 1988).

6 "No one would exchange his country for a foreign land if his own afforded him the means of living a decent and happy life" (Pope Leo XIII, *Rerum Novarum* [*On Capital and Labor*] [May 15, 1891], no. 47. Retrieved from Vatican website: *www.vatican.va)*.

7 Pope Pius XII, *Exsul Familia* (*On the Spiritual Care to Migrants*) (September 30, 1952), in *The Church's Magna Charta for Migrants*, ed. Rev. Giulivo Tessarolo, PSSC (Staten Island, N.Y.: St. Charles Seminary, 1962), 50, citing June 1, 1951, Vatican radio address.

8 Ibid., 51, citing 1948 Vatican letter to U.S. bishops.

9 Pope John XXIII, *Pacem in Terris* (*Peace on Earth*) (April 11, 1963) (Washington, D.C.: USCCB, 1963), no. 25.

10 Pope John Paul II, *Sollicitudo Rei Socialis* (*On Social Concern*) (December 30, 1987) (Washington, D.C.: USCCB, 1988), no. 24.

11 Pontifical Council *Cor Unum* and Pontifical Council for the Pastoral Care of Migrants and Itinerant People, *Refugees: A Challenge to Solidarity* (1992), nos. 13-14. Retrieved from Vatican website: *www.vatican.va*.

12 Pope John Paul II, Message for World Migration Day 1995-1996, *Undocumented Migrants* (July 25, 1995), no. 2. Retrieved from Vatican website: *www.vatican.va*.

13 Pope John Paul II, *Ecclesia in America (The Church in America)* (January 22, 1999) (Washington, D.C.: USCCB, 1999), no. 65, citing *Propositio* 20.

14 "Immigrants from lands across the globe have helped build our great nation. . . . Their presence has enriched our local communities, rural areas, and cities, and their faith in God has enlightened our increasingly secularized culture" (USCCB Resolution on Immigration Reform, November 16, 2000, no. 2).

15 Pope Paul VI, *New Norms for the Care of Migrants "Pastoralis Migratorum"* (August 15, 1969) (Washington, D.C.: USCCB, 1969), no. 7.

16 Pope John Paul II, Message for World Migration Day 1993, *Problems of the Migrant Family* (August 6, 1993), no. 3, citing *Familiaris Consortio*, no. 77. Also see *Welcoming the Stranger Among Us: Unity in Diversity* for recommendations.

17 The bishops in the United States have consistently supported reform of the family reunification visa system. Numerical limits on visas have adversely impacted many nationalities, especially Filipinos. In the context of this statement, we focus on Mexican family reunification because of the proximity of Mexico to the United States and because of the unprecedented number of families separated between these two countries. The per-country limit for Mexico and other affected countries, such as the Philippines, should be increased without harming allotments for other nations.

18 U.S.–Mexico Migration Panel, *Mexico–U.S. Migration: A Shared Responsibility* (Washington, D.C.: Carnegie Endowment for International Peace, 2001). Jeffrey Passel, "New Estimates of the Undocumented Population in the United States" (Washington, D.C.: Migration Policy Institute/Migration Information Source, May 22, 2002).

19 Foro Migraciones, *Migración: México Entre Sus Dos Fronteras, 2000-2001* (México: Foro Migraciones, 2002). The CEM's Human Mobility Commission is a member.

20 In the U.N. Convention, migrant workers are viewed as more than laborers or economic entities. They are social entities with families and, accordingly, have rights, including the right to family reunification. (See International Convention on the Protection of the Rights of All Migrant Workers and Members of Their Families, United Nations General Assembly, December 18, 1990. This document can be obtained from the U.N. Center for Human Rights, 8-14 Avenue de la Paix, 1211 Geneva 10, Switzerland.)

21 In 2000, the U.S. Office of Internal Audit (OIA) of the U.S. Immigration and Naturalization Service (INS) opened 4,527 cases of reported abuse by INS agents. Roughly 10 percent were referred to the U.S. Department of Justice's Civil Rights Division, and less than 10 percent of those referred led to prosecutions. See *Chaos on the U.S.–Mexico Border: A Report on Migration Crossing Deaths, Immigrant Families, and Subsistence-Level Laborers* (Washington, D.C.: Catholic Legal Immigration Network, 2001).

22 The Mexican National Migration Institute has consulting councils for each of its thirty-two regional offices (one for each state and Mexico City) and national office. Such councils include representatives from broad sectors of Mexican society, including universities, shelters, and churches.

23 The U.S. Border Patrol does include some treatment of human rights protection in their training. More intensive instruction in the proper use of force and in appropriate engagement and retention techniques should be considered.

24 In Tecuman, Guatemala, along the Mexico–Guatemala border, smugglers have established offices to receive Central American migrants who wish to travel through Mexico to the United States. (Source: U.S. bishops' delegation to Central America, October 2000.)

25 See *New Slavery, New Freedom: A Pastoral Message on Substance Abuse* (Washington, D.C.: United States Conference of Catholic Bishops, 1990).

26 The law also applies retroactively for an offense committed years ago for which a person has already served his or her sentence.

27 "What article 33 of the Constitution does, is grant the faculty to the government of being able to arbitrarily expel a foreigner. It is arbitrary, firstly, because no due process is required, in other words, it is a faculty that may not be submitted to the scrutiny of constitutionality or legality, either *ex ante* or *ex post*. It is a direct elimination of the guarantees contained under articles 14 and 16 of the Constitution" (Foro Migraciones, *Migración: México Entre Sus Dos Fronteras 2000-2001* [México: Foro Migraciones, 2002], 57).

28 The United States and Canada agreed to coordinate asylum policies on December 5, 2002.

29 U.S.–Mexico Migration Panel, *Mexico–U.S. Migration: A Shared Responsibility* (Washington, D.C.: Carnegie Endowment for International Peace, 2001), 28. Also see *Statistical Yearbook of the Immigration and Naturalization Service, Fiscal Year 2000* (online at *www.ins.usdoj.gov*).

30 The detention of asylum seekers without serious reasons is a violation of the letter and spirit of the "Conclusions on International Protection" of the UNHCR Executive Committee. Both Mexico and the United States are members of the UNHCR Executive Committee, and both have accepted the conclusions. References: No. 44 (XXXVII) 1986; No. 46 (XXVII) 1987; No. 50 (XXXIX), 1988; No. 55 (XL) 1989; No. 65 (XLII) 1991; No. 68 (XLIII) 1992; No. 71 (XLIV) 1993; No. 85 (XLIX) 1998; No. 89 (LI) 2000.

31 Pope John Paul II, *Novo Millennio Ineunte* (January 6, 2001), no. 1. Retrieved from Vatican website: *www.vatican.va*.

32 "Taking the Gospel as its starting-point, a culture of solidarity needs to be promoted, capable of inspiring timely initiatives in support of the poor and the outcast, especially refugees forced to leave their villages and lands in order to flee violence" (EA, no. 52).